People
Around
the
World

Life and Culture in

SOUTH

ASIA

RACHAEL MORLOCK

PowerKiDS
press.

Published in 2021 by The Rosen Publishing Group, Inc.
29 East 21st Street, New York, NY 10010

First Edition

Editor: Siyavush Saidian
Book Design: Seth Hughes

Photo Credits: Cover tscreationz/Shutterstock.com; p. 5 Paula Bronstein/Staff/Getty Images News/Getty Images; p. 7 (left) NurPhoto/Contributor/NurPhoto/Getty Images; p. 7 (right) NOAH SEELAM/Stringer/AFP/Getty Images; p. 7 (bottom) Frank Bienewald/Contributor/LightRocket/Getty Images; p. 9 PRAKASH MATHEMA/Stringer/AFP/Getty Images; p. 11 FARSHAD USYAN/Stringer/AFP/Getty Images; p. 13 NARINDER NANU/Contributor/AFP/Getty Images; p. 14 DIBYANGSHU SARKAR/Contributor/AFP/Getty Images; p. 15 Taylor Weidman/Stringer/Getty Images News/Getty Images; p. 16 LAKRUWAN WANNIARACHCHI/Stringer/AFP/Getty Images; p. 17 Sepia Times/Contributor/Universal Images Group/Getty Images; p. 18 Kunal Rajput/Moment/Getty Images; p. 20 John Moore/Staff/Getty Images News/Getty Images; p. 22 NurPhoto/Contributor/NurPhoto/Getty Images; p. 23 Pictorial Parade/Staff/Archive Photos/Getty Images; p. 24 Themightyquill/Wikimedia Commons; p. 25 Hindustan Times/Contributor/Hindustan Times/Getty Images; p. 26 Paula Bronstein/Staff/Getty Images News/Getty Images; p. 27 Hindustan Times/Contributor/Hindustan Times/Getty Images; p. 28 Buddhika Weerasinghe/Stringer/Getty Images News/Getty Images; p. 30 Hindustan Times/Contributor/Hindustan Times/Getty Images; p. 31 Bettmann/Contributor/Bettmann/Getty Images; p. 33 (top) Digital Light Source/Contributor/Universal Images Group/Getty Images; p. 33 (bottom) Michel GOUNOT/Contributor/Gamma-Rapho/Getty Images; p. 34 Frédéric Soltan/Contributor/Corbis News/Getty Images; p. 35 Angelo Hornak/Contributor/Corbis Historical/Getty Images; p. 37 (top) ASIF HASSAN/Stringer/AFP/Getty Images; p. 37 (bottom) Julian Finney/Staff/Getty Images Sport/Getty Images; p. 39 Marla Aufmuth/Contributor/Getty Images Entertainment/Getty Images; p. 40 Kuni Takahashi/Contributor/Getty Images News/Getty Images; p. 41 Thomas Imo/Contributor/Photothek/Getty Images; p. 42 Education Images/Contributor/Universal Images Group/Getty Images; p. 43 NurPhoto/Contributor/NurPhoto/Getty Images; p. 45 WAKIL KOHSAR/Contributor/AFP/Getty Images.

Cataloging-in-Publication Data

Names: Morlock, Rachael.
Title: Life and culture in South Asia / Rachael Morlock.
Description: New York : PowerKids Press, 2021. | Series: People around the world | Includes glossary and index.
Identifiers: ISBN 9781725321762 (pbk.) | ISBN 9781725321786 (library bound) | ISBN 9781725321779 (6 pack) | ISBN 9781725321793 (ebook)
Subjects: LCSH: South Asia–Juvenile literature. | South Asia–Social life and customs.
Classification: LCC DS335.M67 2021 | DDC 954–dc23

Manufactured in the United States of America

CPSIA Compliance Information: Batch #CSPK20: For Further Information contact Rosen Publishing, New York, New York at 1-800-237-9932

Find us on

Contents

Introduction
AN OVERVIEW OF SOUTH ASIA

A vibrant, **multicultural** society has flourished south of the Himalayan mountains for thousands of years in the region known as South Asia. Around 3000 BC, one of the earliest human civilizations was born here along the fertile banks of the Indus River. The advanced Indus Valley civilization constructed large, organized cities and maintained peaceful settlements. In the 5,000 years since then, South Asians have built on this **legacy** and made significant contributions to world culture.

South Asia is made up of eight nations. From west to east along the Himalayan mountain range, these countries are Afghanistan, Pakistan, India, Nepal, Bangladesh,

The Himalayas, including Mount Everest, are the world's tallest mountains. Historically, they form a natural barrier that once kept the life and culture of South Asia separate from surrounding regions.

and Bhutan. The island nations of Maldives and Sri Lanka in the Indian Ocean to the south are included in the region. South Asia is also called the Indian **subcontinent** because it's distinctly separated from the rest of the Asian continent.

Home to about 1.9 billion people, South Asia is full of life and culture. **Diverse** customs and traditions, religious beliefs, artistic accomplishments, and lifestyles have developed over time. Two of the world's major religions—Hinduism and Buddhism—**originated** in the region. Along with Islam and Christianity, they've shaped culture, politics, the economy, and society for the people of South Asia.

1 RELIGIONS OF SOUTH ASIA

Hinduism developed gradually, probably around the beginning of South Asia's 5,000-year history. Despite its rich history, Hinduism can be a difficult religion to define. It's polytheistic, which means that it recognizes more than one deity. The best-known and most widely worshipped deities are Shiva, Vishnu, and Shakti. Temples to these and other gods and goddesses are built in public and private places for worship.

CULTURAL CONNECTIONS

The Ganges River flows through the fertile plains of India and Bangladesh. It's considered a sacred site for Hindus, and many make **pilgrimages** to **shrines** and temples along the river.

In Hinduism, the god Vishnu can take many forms, including the prankster god Krishna. His blue skin and flute make Krishna a recognizable character in Hindu celebrations and imagery.

Hindus view cows as sacred animals because of their ability to provide life-giving milk. Cows are respected and never eaten by Hindus. Some play a role in rituals and celebrations.

Bathing in the Ganges River is believed to cleanse the souls and bodies of Hindus. After death, some Hindus have their ashes scattered into the river.

Religions of India

RELIGION	PERCENT OF POPULATION
Hinduism	79.8 percent
Islam	14.2 percent
Christianity	2.3 percent
Sikhism	1.7 percent
Buddhism	0.7 percent
Jainism	0.4 percent
Other	0.9 percent

India has many religions, but by far the most widespread is Hinduism.

The Roots of Hinduism

Though religious practices certainly existed in the Indus Valley civilization, they're unknown today. An ancient Indus Valley writing system probably recorded religious beliefs and practices. However, that writing system hasn't yet been **deciphered**. The first-known mention of religion in South Asia appeared after the collapse of the Indus civilization around 1800 BC. At that time, Indo-Europeans called Aryans arrived in the region. The roots of Hinduism are likely a mixture of beliefs from the Indus Valley civilization and a newer religion called Vedism. The Vedas—religious writings from the period of Aryan influence—describe many beliefs that remain central to Hinduism today.

Unlike many other religions, Hinduism doesn't have a known founder or a central organization that oversees the practices of believers. Instead, Hinduism is more of a personal and spiritual philosophy. It's based on a tolerance for other beliefs and the idea that all religions come from one source of spiritual truth. Hinduism also maintains the idea of a cycle called samsara. Through this cycle, the soul is reborn after death in a process called **reincarnation**.

Reincarnation is also a feature of the second religion to grow out of South Asia: Buddhism.

reincarnation: Rebirth into new forms of life.

Colorful prayer flags at a Buddhist temple in Nepal blow in the wind, sending blessings into the world. You can usually identify the Buddhist monks nearby by their robes.

Sometime around the sixth century BC, a prince named Siddhartha Gautama was born near the Himalayan mountains. As an adult, Siddhartha left behind his worldly possessions in order to help others and seek the meaning of life. Buddhist tradition claims that Siddhartha meditated under a tree for 40 days until he achieved **enlightenment**. He became known as Buddha, or "awakened one," as he traveled through India sharing his new knowledge and wisdom with others. His followers have grown and spread around the world since then.

Jainism

After Hinduism and Buddhism, Jainism is the third religion that originated from South Asia. Jainism was founded around the sixth century AD. It teaches that enlightenment can be reached through ahimsa, or a life of nonviolence in thoughts, speech, and actions. Jains believe that all living things have souls, including plants and animals. They show respect for others and nonviolence through strict vegetarian diets. Jain followers, monks, and nuns worship in temples, live simple lives, and practice self-discipline and meditation. Unlike Hinduism and Buddhism, Jainism wasn't widely adopted outside South Asia. Nevertheless, it's one of the oldest religions practiced in India today.

Different branches of Buddhism developed in Sri Lanka, Nepal, and Bhutan in South Asia. These branches are united by the practices of nonviolence and meditation taught by the Buddha as a path toward **nirvana**.

Islam—South Asia's third major religion—was carried into the region by

CULTURAL CONNECTIONS

Sikhism, founded in the 15th century AD, is one of the newer religions in South Asia. Its practices are often seen as a bridge between Islam and Hinduism.

Muslims from the northwest. It began to take root in the eighth century AD, when Muslim armies spread their beliefs through Afghanistan, Pakistan, and India. Unlike Hinduism, Islam is a monotheistic religion that only recognizes one god. The Qur'an is Islam's primary religious text. Filled with instructions given to the prophet Muhammad, it guides believers in daily life and worship. Islam is most common in Afghanistan, Pakistan, and Bangladesh.

Men kneel in prayer outside the Blue **Mosque** *in Mazar-e-Sharif, Afghanistan. Muslims pray five times throughout the day in a practice that connects them to other Muslims around the world.*

mosque: A building that is used for Muslim religious services.

2 COLORFUL FESTIVALS

Throughout the year in South Asia, the calendar is filled with celebrations of religious and national holidays. All of the nations of South Asia were under British or other foreign control at some point in their history. Each country's successful independence movement is celebrated as a national holiday. Most other holidays are linked to Hinduism, Islam, Buddhism, and other religious traditions.

CULTURAL CONNECTIONS

Gandhi Jayanti is a national Indian holiday that celebrates Mohandas Gandhi's birthday on October 2, 1869. Gandhi led the nonviolent movement that resulted in Indian independence from Britain in 1947.

Followers of multiple religions celebrate Diwali, India's biggest holiday. It takes place over five days in late October or early November. This festival celebrates the triumph of light and goodness over dark forces. In Hinduism, Diwali takes on different regional meanings. North Indians celebrate the victories of King Rama, South Indians honor Krishna's successes, and West Indians remember the triumphs of Lord Vishnu. Jains, Sikhs, and Buddhists also use the occasion to mark important moments in their own religious history. All Diwali celebrations share the tradition of lighting clay pots filled with oil. These are arranged in rows in homes and temples or released into rivers.

In the Sikh tradition, Diwali celebrates **Guru** *Hargobind's return from prison in 1619. The Sikh gurus were spiritual leaders and teachers who helped build up and spread Sikhism.*

guru: A religious and spiritual teacher.

Holi

Holi is a colorful and lively Hindu festival that's celebrated throughout South Asia. It's especially significant in India, Nepal, and Sri Lanka, where businesses close and the streets fill with people of all backgrounds. The festival marks the beginning of spring, and it starts with a bonfire. This fire marks the story of a Hindu prince called Prahlada and the triumph of good over evil. The next day, as the land begins to bloom with flowers, the streets and people are painted with tinted water and brightly colored powders called *gulal*. People sing, dance, exchange blessings, and eat festive foods together.

Women in Kolkata, India, celebrate the beginning of spring as a season of hope. Participants smudge and throw colorful powders on each other as part of the Holi festival.

Most Buddhist holidays and festivals are centered on important events in the Buddha's life. Wesak is the primary Buddhist holiday. It celebrates the birth, enlightenment, and death of the Buddha. All three events are said to have taken place during the full moon in May, which is when Wesak is observed. Buddhists visit temples on this day, chant hymns, and pour water over the shoulders of Buddhist sculptures. This cleansing is a reminder for followers to **purify** their inner thoughts.

The Tenchi Festival takes place in Lo Manthang, Nepal, to ceremonially drive evil spirits from the area. Buddhist monks chant prayers, play traditional horns and drums, and perform ritual dances.

Folk Dances

Music and dance are essential to South Asian festivals. Many regional folk dances have ancient roots and are a form of theater. Indian dancers use certain gestures, costumes, and songs to tell stories, often about Hindu gods. Ritual dances are also a part of national culture in Sri Lanka, Pakistan, and Bangladesh. In Sri Lanka, *kandyan* is a national dance that tells stories of kings, heroes, and gods. The *khattak* dance in Pakistan has been passed down by the Pashtun people, a tribal mountain community. Its energetic steps are performed by men wearing traditional clothing and carrying rifles or swords.

Kandyan dancers perform and celebrate Navam Perahera in Colombo, Sri Lanka. In this annual festival, monks, dancers, and elephants parade through Colombo around a Buddhist temple called Gangaramaya.

Muslim holidays similarly relate to events in the prophet Muhammad's life. The **revelation** of the words of the Qur'an to Muhammad is remembered during Ramadan. This is a month of prayer and fasting for Muslims, who don't eat from sunrise to sunset. Ramadan ends with the new moon on the night of Chaand Raat and is followed by a day of prayer and celebration called Eid al-Fitr. Eid al-Adha is another important Muslim holiday that honors

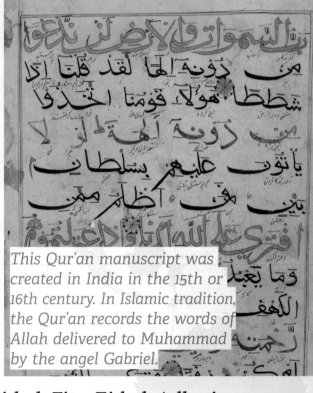

This Qur'an manuscript was created in India in the 15th or 16th century. In Islamic tradition, the Qur'an records the words of Allah delivered to Muhammad by the angel Gabriel.

the story of the prophet Abraham. This holiday occurs at the end of the hajj, the period of time each year when Muslims make pilgrimages to the holy city of **Mecca**.

In Pakistan, India, and Bangladesh, Muslim women paint their hands with **henna** *tattoos for Chaand Raat.*

3 ETHNICITY AND SOCIETY

In addition to religion, South Asian culture is also shaped by a diversity of **ethnic** and social identities. In the harsh landscape of Afghanistan, natural barriers have largely kept ethnic groups separate and distinct from each other through history. Tajik and Uzbek people live in northern Afghanistan. Pashtun people are found in southern Afghanistan and make up the largest ethnic group in the nation. The Hazara live in the central highlands of Afghanistan. They're especially separated from other ethnic groups since they're Shia Muslims in an area where Sunni Islam is the majority religion. Tensions between these Afghan ethnic groups have led to violence in the region.

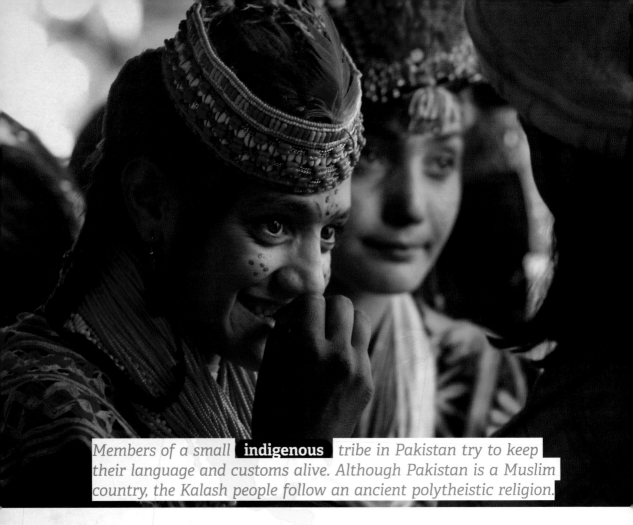

*Members of a small **indigenous** tribe in Pakistan try to keep their language and customs alive. Although Pakistan is a Muslim country, the Kalash people follow an ancient polytheistic religion.*

The largest ethnicity in Pakistan is the Punjabi group, which accounts for almost half of the country's population. Pashtun people are the second-largest group and live near the northwestern border with Afghanistan. Sindhi people are mostly found in southern Pakistan, and Baluchis cover a small area on the Indian border. Hazara and other small minority groups also live in Pakistan. Conflict in Pakistan has arisen as large groups of Afghan **refugees** have moved to Pakistan in the past few decades.

CULTURAL CONNECTIONS

The Lhotshampa are an ethnic group in Bhutan with ties to Nepal. Beginning in 1989, many Lhotshampa people became refugees. They were forced out of Bhutan because of their Nepalese ancestry.

The Hindu community in South Asia is a vast collection of people with different ethnic backgrounds. However, the most notable social divisions are based on class rather than ethnicity. Ancient Hindu beliefs included the idea of *varnas*, or social groups based

BRAHMIN
priests

KSHATRIYA
warriors, kings

VAISHYA
merchants, landowners

SUDRA
commoners, peasants, servants

UNTOUCHABLE, OUTCASTE, OUT OF CASTE
street sweepers, latrine cleaners

Ancient Hinduism taught about four varnas, organized from highest to lowest social status. Originally, varnas were assigned based on individual skills and qualities. They changed over time into **hereditary** *castes.*

Sunni and Shia

Two main forms of Islam are practiced in South Asia: Sunni and Shia. Islam split after Muhammad's death when the two groups disagreed over who their new leader should be. Although they still share basic beliefs, Sunni and Shia Muslims have developed different practices over time. Sunni is the majority branch in South Asia and is more **conservative** than Shia. In Afghanistan, 99.7 percent of the country is Muslim, but only about 10 percent of that group is Shia. The numbers are similar in Pakistan. As a result, Shia Muslims are sometimes the target of violence and **discrimination**.

on occupation. Subgroups within the varnas are called *jati*. Over time, this social **hierarchy** developed into a caste system that was determined by birth. Hindus were born into ranked, fixed groups, called castes. They were expected to marry, work, and socialize within their caste.

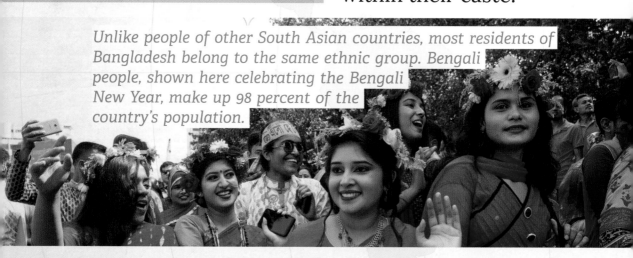

Unlike people of other South Asian countries, most residents of Bangladesh belong to the same ethnic group. Bengali people, shown here celebrating the Bengali New Year, make up 98 percent of the country's population.

Ethnic groups are distinct and important to identity in Nepal. The Chhetri ethnic group is the largest. The Magar ethnic group is one of the oldest ethnicities in Nepal. Sherpas have gained international attention for their mountaineering skills.

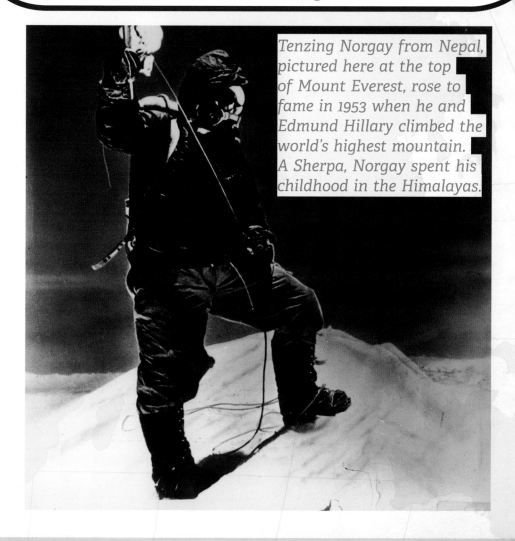

Tenzing Norgay from Nepal, pictured here at the top of Mount Everest, rose to fame in 1953 when he and Edmund Hillary climbed the world's highest mountain. A Sherpa, Norgay spent his childhood in the Himalayas.

The Partition of India

After India gained independence from Britain in 1947, it was divided into West Pakistan, India, and East Pakistan. (In 1971, East Pakistan became Bangladesh.) This division, called a partition, led to the mass **migration** of more than 10 million people. Muslims in India moved to Pakistan, and Hindus in Pakistan moved to India. These shifting religious groups account for the fact that Pakistan and Bangladesh today have Muslim majorities while India is primarily Hindu. Conflict arose in Punjab, an area that was divided by the partition's western border. The Kashmir region has also been the subject of conflict, claimed by both Pakistan and India.

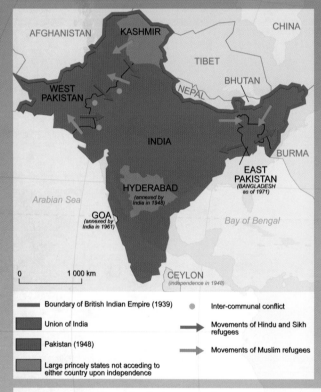

AFGHANISTAN
KASHMIR
CHINA
TIBET
BHUTAN
WEST PAKISTAN
NEPAL
INDIA
BURMA
EAST PAKISTAN (BANGLADESH as of 1971)
HYDERABAD (annexed by India in 1948)
Arabian Sea
GOA (annexed by India in 1961)
Bay of Bengal
0   1 000 km
CEYLON (independence in 1948)

- ▬ Boundary of British Indian Empire (1939)
- ⬛ Union of India
- ⬛ Pakistan (1948)
- ⬛ Large princely states not acceding to either country upon independence
- ● Inter-communal conflict
- → Movements of Hindu and Sikh refugees
- → Movements of Muslim refugees

Millions of South Asians migrated into and out of Pakistan after the partition of India. "Pakistan" is an acronym with letters from local provinces: "p" from Punjab, "a" from Afghania, "k" from Kashmir, "I" from Indus-Sind, and "stan" from Baluchistan.

migration: Movement from one region to another.

Many South Asians are still impacted by the caste system, especially in India. The Indian constitution outlawed some discrimination based on caste and allowed people to move more freely through social classes. However, discrimination still exists for many low-caste members. This is especially true for the "untouchable" caste. Members of this group fall below the caste system as outcasts. They have traditionally been given jobs that are

Students in New Delhi protest the mistreatment of Dalits and call for new protective laws. The word "Dalit" means "broken people" and refers to a long history of oppression against untouchables.

considered unpleasant and unclean. Members of this group have adopted the name "Dalit" and called for greater equality in Indian society.

4 LANGUAGE AND LITERATURE

I n addition to being ethnically distinct, many of the peoples and provinces of South Asia also have unique languages and **dialects**. These can be divided into two main groups: Indo-Aryan and Dravidian. Ancient languages have evolved over time into the forms most spoken in South Asia today.

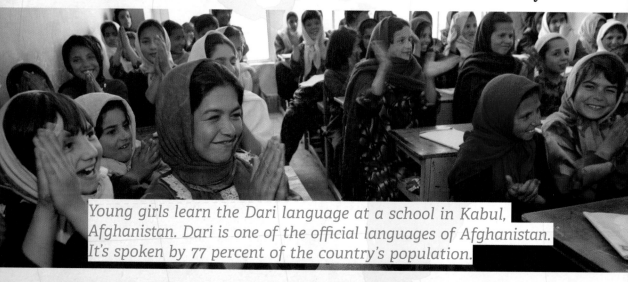

Young girls learn the Dari language at a school in Kabul, Afghanistan. Dari is one of the official languages of Afghanistan. It's spoken by 77 percent of the country's population.

dialect: A form of language spoken in a certain area that uses some of its own words, grammar, and pronunciations.

Historically, the primary Indo-Aryan language of the region was Sanskrit. It took over with the arrival of Indo-Aryan peoples from the northwest. Vedic Sanskrit evolved in northern India, and the first written example is dated to about 1500 BC. Around AD 1000, new Indo-Aryan forms began to develop into the languages spoken today. These include Hindi, Punjabi, Sindhi, Bengali, and other regional languages and dialects in Pakistan, northern India, Nepal, and Bangladesh. Their vocabulary was influenced over time by Arabic from Muslim invaders and English from British **colonizers**.

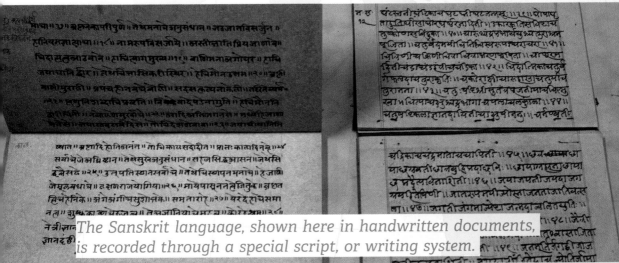

The Sanskrit language, shown here in handwritten documents, is recorded through a special script, or writing system.

The Vedas and the Upanishads

The Vedas are sacred Hindu texts that were first collected between 1500 and 1000 BC. They contain important ideas that are central to Hinduism. For example, the varnas are described in the Rigveda, the oldest text of the Vedas. The Upanishads were written between 800 and 500 BC in India and lay out the concepts of dharma, karma, and samsara. Dharma is the duty to perform moral acts. Karma measures whether actions are good or bad. Samsara is the cycle of rebirth, and it's decided by karma. The Upanishads also describe how to escape samsara and reach enlightenment, or moksha.

The second ancient language group in South Asia is called Dravidian. Its origin is unknown and separate from that of Indo-Aryan languages. The Dravidian language family is mostly found today in southern India and Sri Lanka. It includes Tamil, Telegu, Malayalam, and Kannada.

A man in Jaffna, Sri Lanka, reads a Tamil newspaper. Tamil is a Dravidian language spoken in southern India and Sri Lanka. About 28 percent of Sri Lankan citizens speak Tamil.

With huge numbers of native speakers, Hindi, Bangla, and Punjabi are ranked among the most spoken languages in the world. About 425 million people speak Hindi as their first language.

Some of the most historically and religiously significant literature of South Asia was written in Sanskrit. Vedic Sanskrit is connected to early holy texts called the Vedas. These are important writings in Hinduism, and they continue to be read in their original language. As Sanskrit changed and evolved, it became the language of sacred **scriptures** and hymns in Jainism, Buddhism, and Sikhism.

Languages of South Asia

COUNTRY	PRIMARY LANGUAGES SPOKEN
Afghanistan	Dari, Pashto, Uzbek
Bangladesh	Bangla, English
Bhutan	Sharchhopka, Dzongkha, Lhotshamkha
India	Hindi, Bengali, Telugu, Morathi, Tamil, Urdu, Gujarati, Kannada, Malayalam, Oriya, Punjabi, Assamese, Maithili, English
Maldives	Dhiveti, English
Nepal	Nepali, Maithali, Bhojpun, Tharu, Tamang, Newar, Magar, Bajjika, Urdu, Avadhi, Limbu, Gurung
Pakistan	Punjabi, Sindhi, English
Sri Lanka	Sinhala, Tamil, English

It's estimated that between 300 and 1,000 languages are spoken throughout the South Asian region.

scripture: The sacred writings of a religion.

The tales of the Ramayana are often retold as plays and dances. They show how Prince Rama rescued his wife, Sita, from the evil King Ravana.

Sanskrit is also the language of two **epic poems** about India. The first, the *Ramayana*, was composed sometime around 500 BC by the poet Valmiki. It follows the life and adventures of Prince Rama. The second epic work is the *Mahabharata* from about 400 BC, which tells the story of two branches of a family struggling for power. Hindus believe the story contains important philosophical teachings about dharma, or moral laws.

CULTURAL CONNECTIONS

The *Bhagavad Gita* is a sacred scripture within the *Mahabharata*. It describes many of the core teachings of Hinduism through a conversation between Prince Arjuna and Krishna, an **avatar** for Vishnu.

epic poem: A long poem that tells the story of one or more heroic characters.

A Place in World Literature

Many authors have introduced the world to South Asian culture and gained international acclaim for their writing. Salman Rushdie is an Indian writer whose stories focus on life in the Indian subcontinent and explore religion and politics. Arundhati Roy is another Indian writer whose novel *The God of Small Things* earned her the Man Booker Prize in 1998. Michael Ondaatje was born in Sri Lanka, and his book *Running in the Family* talks about life on the island. Samrat Upadhyay is the first author from Nepal to write in English and have books published in the United States.

The importance of literature in South Asia has continued from ancient texts to modern-day writing. Literature varies regionally and nationally in language and style. However, many modern works are written in or translated into English and read widely around the world.

In 1913, Rabindranath Tagore became the first Asian author to be awarded the Nobel Prize for literature. Tagore was Bengali and born in India. He wrote inventive poetry, essays, plays, and short stories.

5

ARTISTIC HERITAGE

Like all aspects of South Asian culture, regional art is closely tied to religious traditions. The earliest art of the Indus Valley included small seals decorated with animal figures. Some ancient sculptures also survive, but most historic South Asian art begins with the rise of Hinduism, Buddhism, and Jainism.

Buddhist art takes shape in temples, sculptures, and paintings. Stone Buddhist temples with domed tops are called stupas. They generally contain relics—often ashes—of the Buddha. Temples are often decorated with sculptures and wall paintings that illustrate the life of the Buddha.

CULTURAL CONNECTIONS

Artists have had an honored place in South Asian society throughout history. The arts were enthusiastically promoted during the Gupta period during the fourth and fifth century AD in the Indian subcontinent.

India's Ajanta Caves are an example of rock-cut architecture, with temples and sculptures carved into a cliffside. They also contain India's oldest wall paintings.

Buddhist Mandalas

High in the Himalayan Mountains of Nepal, Buddhist monks create detailed designs called mandalas. The act of making a mandala is a religious experience that's often accompanied by prayers and chanting from other monks. Mandalas can be formed as paintings or as three-dimensional works. Raised hills and plains are carefully shaped out of colored grains of sand. The sand comes together in a complicated circular and geometric design. After the monks have completed their work within hours—or even days—they wipe the sand away and destroy the mandala. This symbolic act is a reminder that nothing is permanent.

Buddhist monks in Nepal grind rocks from the nearby Himalayan Mountains to make the colored sand used in mandalas. The sand is scraped through small copper funnels onto the design.

A Hindu temple follows a similar construction style and is also made from stone. A temple is dedicated to a certain god or gods as a place where worshippers can interact with them. The outer walls are often carved with sculptural figures and decorations. Inside the temple, an inner chamber contains a statue of the honored god. A tall tower reaches into the heavens above the statue chamber.

The Elephanta Caves on a small island near Mumbai, India, are dedicated to Shiva. The god is shown with three heads that represent, from left to right: destruction, harmony, and creation in the cycle of life.

South Asian painting and sculpture are mainly focused on human and animal figures. They feature bodies that are mostly realistic but also have a rounded quality that gives them an otherworldly, spiritual sense. This style is seen in paintings and sculptures that tell the stories of gods. Paintings use shading to give figures depth and presence. Within painted or sculptural Hindu art, gods have certain features, gestures, and tokens that make their identities recognizable.

In this painting from the 13th century, the goddess Durga battles a demon. Her many arms and the lion she rides into the fight help worshippers identify her.

Bollywood

Amidst the ancient and religious works of South Asia, there's one truly modern art form. Bollywood is the name for India's huge film industry. It was launched in the 1930s. Now, Bollywood produces hundreds of sweeping dramas and family-friendly romances every year. One of the most important features of Bollywood movies is song and dance routines with colorful costumes. Most Bollywood movies are in major Indian languages that are accessible to people around the country. This popular art form is a celebration of Indian culture, and it's enjoyed in India, Pakistan, and many other parts of South Asia and the world.

Islamic art traditionally avoids **depicting** humans or animals. Instead, Muslim art in South Asia is decorated with abstract shapes, plant forms, and geometric patterns. Calligraphy, or detailed artistic writing, is a common element in Islamic art. Colored or painted tiles also decorate the walls and floors of mosques. Like Hindu and Buddhist temples, large domes and towers typically top mosque architecture.

CULTURAL CONNECTIONS

It wasn't until the Islamic period, starting in AD 1200, that paper became widely available in South Asia. Paper replaced palm leaves and allowed artists to create more lasting and detailed paintings.

The Shah Jahan Mosque in Thatta, Pakistan, showcases the decorative patterns and colorful tiles that are a **hallmark** of Islamic art and architecture.

The Taj Mahal in Agra, India, is one of South Asia's most recognizable monuments. This white marble tomb is a mighty work of Islamic art built between 1632 and 1647.

hallmark: A distinct characteristic of something, such as an art style.

Overall, South Asian artists have created a fairly unified style of art. Although they've mixed in influences from other world regions, such as the Middle East and Britain, they've also maintained a distinct South Asian identity. Artists in the modern age are free to experiment with global styles and find new ways of expanding South Asian art.

6 DAILY LIFE

Just like in other parts of the world, school, work, and time with friends and family are part of daily life in South Asia. However, while almost all children in Sri Lanka are enrolled in school, other countries struggle to provide education. About 11 percent of children aren't educated in South Asia. A number of factors–including

Malala Yousafzai is a Pakistani activist who became the youngest recipient of the Nobel Peace Prize in 2014. She fights to earn equal access to education for girls and all children around the world.

climate challenges, poverty, caste and gender discrimination, and political conflict—make education a complicated challenge. In this region, girls are less likely than boys to attend school. Girls in Pakistan and Afghanistan, especially, face strict social and religious rules that may keep them out of the classroom. As countries work to close the gender education gap, they must also battle wider discrimination against girls and women.

Students gather for prayer at a school in Bhutan. Monasteries have been a traditional source of education throughout South Asian history. Today, the governments of South Asia work toward providing educational opportunities for all children.

In poor South Asian communities, many young people leave school early or never attend in order to support their families. More than 41 million children—ages 5 to 14—work as laborers in the region. Farmwork is the most common form of employment for children, as agriculture is a major occupation for people in the region. More than 751 million people in South Asia—or about 55 percent of the population—depend on farming for their livelihood. Crops such as rice, wheat, tea, and fruits grow in the area.

In addition to rural farming communities, city life is big and growing in South Asia. New Delhi, India, is the largest city in the region and one of the largest in the world.

Flavors of South Asia

Religious rules govern many South Asian diets. Hindus don't eat cows, Muslims don't eat pigs, Jains don't eat any meat, and many other Hindus and Buddhists follow strict vegetarian diets. Rice is a common food and a staple in countries such as Bangladesh. The flavorful spices that grow across South Asia are typically mixed in with any meal. Curry powder is especially popular in Indian dishes. It's made from a mixture of spices including turmeric, chili, coriander, cumin, ginger, and pepper. The spices add flavor to an abundance of meat and vegetarian dishes.

Bright, colorful spices are lined up for sale at a market in Goa, India. Different spices are often mixed together and used for medicine or to season rice, vegetables, and meat.

South Asia is often in danger of natural disasters and extreme weather. Every year, **monsoon** winds sweep across the region from the southwest, carrying heavy rains from the Indian Ocean. These rains lead to flooding that can destroy farms and weaken cities. Drought and heat waves are other common regional problems. **Typhoons** and **tsunamis** threaten coastal areas, and **earthquakes** are especially dangerous in the mountains. The people of South Asia must adapt to the changing weather and natural disasters that make life in the region difficult.

Some of the worst effects of monsoon winds are felt in Bangladesh. Flooding causes landslides and damage to farms. Cities such as Bangladesh's capital, Dhaka, also suffer.

However, the natural world is also a source of pride and identity in South Asia. The stunning beauty of the Himalayas and other natural wonders are important to life in the area. Over thousands of years, natural forces and human

Traditional Clothing

Clothing styles vary in South Asia and are often related to religious beliefs. Women in Afghanistan, Pakistan, and other Muslim communities commonly wear head coverings. Islamic law requires both men and women to dress modestly, and clothing is generally long and loose-fitting. Hindu women in India, Sri Lanka, Nepal, and Bangladesh wear traditional saris. Saris are made from a long piece of colorful or finely decorated fabric, draped over the body. Men's clothing in the region includes long skirts or loose pants and tunic tops. Sikh men can be recognized by their turbans, and Buddhist monks and nuns can often be spotted in traditional yellow or red robes.

creativity have contributed to the diverse **cultural landscapes** of South Asia. Religious, ethnic, and artistic histories have shaped a culturally unique and remarkable region of the world.

An extreme Islamic group called the Taliban came to power in Afghanistan in 1996 and outlawed kite flying. The end of Taliban control in 2001 meant Afghans could fly their kites again.

GLOSSARY

avatar: The embodiment of a god in human form.

conservative: Tending to stick to traditional ideas.

decipher: To convert into an understandable form.

discrimination: Unfair treatment of people because of their race or beliefs.

diverse: Different or varied.

hierarchy: A system that places people in a series of levels with varying importance or status.

legacy: Something that has been handed down.

oppression: The unjust use of power over another; treating people in a cruel or unfair way.

originate: To come into existence.

pilgrimage: A journey to a sacred place.

purify: To cleanse.

revelation: An act of revealing divine truth.

FOR MORE INFORMATION

BOOKS:

Brennan, Katy. *Buddhism*. New York: Britannica Educational Publishing, 2019.

Singh, Rina. *Diwali: Festival of Lights*. Victoria, Canada: Orca Book Publishers, 2016.

Yousafzai, Malala. *I Am Malala: How One Girl Stood Up for Education and Changed the World*. Farmington Hills, MI: Thorndike Press, 2018.

WEBSITES:

Buddhism: Basic Beliefs
uri.org/kids/world-religions/buddhist-beliefs
This site offers readers information about Buddhism, one of South Asia's most popular and unique religions.

Celebrating Ramadan
kids.nationalgeographic.com/explore/history/ramadan
Colorful pictures and descriptions bring Ramadan and its traditions to life on this site.

India for Kids
www.kids-world-travel-guide.com/india-for-kids.html
On this site, you can learn more about India, the largest and most populated country in South Asia.

INDEX